UNVELING
THE WORLD OF

ONE PIECE

DECODING THE CHARACTERS, THEMES, AND WORLD OF THE ANIME

-

CREATED BY

ETERNIA PUBLISHING

ETERNIA
PUBLISHING

Unveling The World Of One Piece: Decoding The
Characters, Themes, And World Of The Anime
By Eternia Publishing and Zander Pearce

Author: Eternia Publishing and Zander Pearce
Contact: contact@eterniapublishing.com

CONTENT

INTRODUCTION

One Piece is a beloved anime that has captured the hearts of millions of fans around the world. With its richly detailed world, complex characters, and epic storyline, it's no wonder that so many people have been drawn into the world of the Straw Hat Pirates. However, for those who are new to the series or even for those who have been following it for years, it can be difficult to fully understand the many layers of the story.

That's where this companion guide comes in. **"Unveling The World Of One Piece"** is a comprehensive guide to the anime that will help fans better understand the many themes, characters, and plotlines of this amazing series. This guide is designed for fans who want to take a deeper dive into the world of One Piece, and discover the many hidden meanings and references that make the series so unique.

THE WORLD OF ONE PIECE: AN INTRODUCTION TO THE SERIES

One Piece is a Japanese manga series created by Eiichiro Oda that has captivated audiences around the world. The series began serialization in 1997 and has since become a cultural phenomenon, with over 1 billion copies of the manga in circulation and a long-running anime adaptation that has aired over 1000 episodes.

The world of One Piece takes place in a fictional world where pirates rule the seas and the search for the ultimate treasure, known as the One Piece, is the driving force for many characters. The protagonist, Monkey D. Luffy, is a young pirate with rubber powers who is determined to become the Pirate King and find the One Piece.

As Luffy and his crew, the Straw Hat Pirates, journey through the world, they encounter a diverse cast of characters, each with their own unique motivations and abilities. From devil fruit users with fantastical powers to cyborgs and fishmen, the world of One Piece is full of colorful and exciting characters.

In addition to the diverse characters, the world of One Piece is richly detailed and full of fascinating lore. The series takes place in a vast world of islands, each with their own distinct culture and history. The World Government, a powerful entity that controls much of the world, is constantly at odds with pirates and other factions seeking to challenge their authority.

One of the defining features of One Piece is its themes of friendship, perseverance, and adventure. Luffy's crew is a tight-knit group that supports and encourages each other through thick and thin, and their bonds are often tested as they face tough challenges and powerful enemies.

The world of One Piece is a rich and exciting universe that has captured the hearts of fans around the world. Whether you're a long-time fan or just getting started, there's always something new and exciting to discover in the world of One Piece.

THE HISTORY AND EVOLUTION OF ONE PIECE

One Piece has a rich history and has evolved significantly since its inception. The manga was first published in Weekly Shonen Jump in 1997, and the anime adaptation began airing in 1999. Since then, the series has grown into a cultural phenomenon with a massive global following.

The story of One Piece is set in a world of pirates, where the search for the ultimate treasure, known as the One Piece, is the driving force for many characters. The series follows the journey of Monkey D. Luffy, a young pirate with rubber powers, as he assembles a crew and sets out to become the Pirate King.

One Piece has become known for its expansive world-building, intricate plot, and colorful characters. The series has introduced countless unique characters and locations, each with its own backstory and lore. Additionally, the world of One Piece is constantly expanding, with new islands, factions, and characters being introduced regularly.

Over the years, the anime adaptation has undergone significant changes. The animation and art style have improved significantly since the show's inception, and the anime has adapted numerous arcs from the manga. The anime has also added filler episodes and arcs, which are original stories not found in the manga.

In addition to the anime, One Piece has also been adapted into video games, movies, and merchandise. The franchise has been incredibly successful, with over 1 billion copies of the manga in circulation and a long-running anime adaptation that has aired over 1000 episodes.

One Piece has also become known for its themes of friendship, perseverance, and adventure. The series has inspired a passionate fanbase, and its impact can be seen in the countless pieces of fan art, cosplay, and fanfiction that have been created.

The history and evolution of One Piece have been marked by constant growth and expansion. The series has become a cultural phenomenon that has captured the hearts of fans around the world and shows no signs of slowing down anytime soon.

THE CULTURAL REFERENCES IN ONE PIECE: A DEEP DIVE

One Piece is a Japanese manga series that is known for its expansive world-building and intricate plot, filled with unique characters and locations. One of the elements that make One Piece so unique is its use of cultural references throughout the story.

Throughout the series, author Eiichiro Oda has drawn inspiration from a variety of cultural sources. For example, the series features characters based on real-life historical figures, such as Edward Teach (also known as Blackbeard) and Bartholomew Roberts. Additionally, the series includes references to various cultures, such as the Viking-inspired warriors of Elbaf and the samurai of Wano Country.

One of the most prominent cultural references in One Piece is its use of Western mythology and folklore. For example, the series features characters such as Enel, who is based on the god of thunder in Norse mythology, and the Gorgon sisters, who are based on the mythological creatures of the same name.

Another prominent cultural reference in One Piece is its use of Japanese mythology and culture. The series introduces several characters and locations inspired by Japanese folklore and history. For example, the island of Dressrosa is based on Spain, and many of its characters have Spanish names and attire, while the country of Wano is heavily inspired by feudal Japan.

One Piece also includes several references to pop culture and other media. For example, the character of Brook is a reference to the musician James Brown, while the character of Franky is based on the robot from the Japanese manga series Tetsujin 28-go.

The use of cultural references in One Piece adds depth and richness to the world and characters. These references allow readers and viewers to make connections to real-life history, mythology, and culture, while also providing a unique and engaging storytelling experience.

THE CREATION AND DEVELOPMENT OF ONE PIECE'S CHARACTERS

The characters of One Piece are some of the most iconic in the world of manga and anime. From the main protagonist, Monkey D. Luffy, to the many side characters that populate the world of One Piece, each character is unique, with their own backstory, personality, and motivations.

The creation and development of these characters is largely the work of author Eiichiro Oda. Oda has stated in interviews that he spends a significant amount of time developing each character, with the goal of making each one unique and memorable.

When creating a new character, Oda often starts with a basic concept, such as a specific personality trait or skill. He then builds on this foundation, adding details such as physical appearance and backstory. Oda also puts significant effort into designing each character's outfit, often drawing inspiration from real-life fashion and historical clothing.

One of the defining features of One Piece's characters is their unique abilities and powers. Many characters in the series have eaten devil fruits, which grant them superhuman abilities. Oda has stated that he spends a significant amount of time designing these powers, often drawing inspiration from mythology, science fiction, and other sources.

The development of the characters in One Piece is an ongoing process, with many characters undergoing significant growth and change over the course of the series. Oda has stated that he puts a lot of effort into developing each character's backstory and motivations, as well as their relationships with other characters in the story.

The creation and development of the characters in One Piece is a labor of love for author Eiichiro Oda. Through his dedication and attention to detail, he has created a rich and engaging cast of characters that have captivated audiences around the world.

THE SIGNIFICANCE OF NAMES AND SYMBOLS IN ONE PIECE

In the world of One Piece, names and symbols carry significant meaning and play a crucial role in the story. The series is filled with characters and locations that have unique and meaningful names, as well as symbols that represent important concepts and themes.

One of the most significant uses of names in One Piece is the naming of characters. Each character's name is carefully chosen by author Eiichiro Oda to reflect their personality, abilities, and backstory. For example, the main protagonist, Monkey D. Luffy, is named after the monkey king Sun Wukong from the Chinese classic Journey to the West, while the character Nico Robin's name is derived from the Greek myth of the robin, a bird associated with good luck.

Symbols also play an important role in One Piece. The most prominent symbol in the series is the pirate flag, which represents the crew's identity and values. Each crew has its own unique flag, with symbols and designs that reflect their personality and goals. For example, the Straw Hat Pirates' flag features a skull wearing a straw hat, which represents their captain, Luffy.

Additionally, One Piece features several recurring symbols that represent important concepts and themes in the story. For example, the three-eyed skull symbol, which represents the Will of D, a mysterious and powerful force that is tied to the world's history and the main character's journey.

The use of names and symbols in One Piece adds depth and richness to the story, allowing readers and viewers to make connections and draw meaning from the world and characters. These names and symbols also help to build a sense of continuity and coherence in the story, tying together the many threads and themes that run throughout the series.

The significance of names and symbols in One Piece is a testament to author Eiichiro Oda's attention to detail and his commitment to creating a rich and engaging storytelling experience.

THE ROLE OF DEVIL FRUITS AND HAKI IN ONE PIECE

In the world of One Piece, Devil Fruits and Haki are two of the most important concepts that define the abilities and powers of the characters. These two concepts play a critical role in the story, shaping the characters' abilities and strategies in battle, as well as the overall plot and themes of the series.

Devil Fruits are a type of fruit found throughout the world of One Piece that grant their consumers unique and often powerful abilities. These abilities can range from the ability to control fire, to the power to transform into a giant or an animal. However, eating a Devil Fruit comes with a significant drawback: the consumer loses the ability to swim, and becomes vulnerable to drowning.

Haki, on the other hand, is a special power that certain characters can use to enhance their physical abilities and sense the presence of others. There are three types of Haki: Observation Haki, which allows characters to sense the presence of others and predict their movements; Armament Haki, which allows characters to coat their body or weapons with a powerful armor-like substance; and Conqueror's Haki, which allows characters to intimidate and control others with their presence.

The role of Devil Fruits and Haki in One Piece is significant, as they shape the abilities and strategies of the characters, as well as the overall plot and themes of the series. The powers and abilities granted by Devil Fruits allow characters to perform incredible feats and overcome seemingly impossible challenges, while the use of Haki in battles adds a strategic element to combat.

Moreover, the themes of power, ambition, and responsibility are closely tied to the concepts of Devil Fruits and Haki. The acquisition and use of these powers often come with significant consequences, and characters must weigh the benefits against the risks of using them.

The role of Devil Fruits and Haki in One Piece is a critical part of the series, shaping the abilities and strategies of the characters, as well as the overall plot and themes of the story.

THE IMPORTANCE OF FRIENDSHIP AND LOYALTY IN ONE PIECE

One of the most prominent themes in One Piece is the importance of friendship and loyalty. The series is filled with examples of characters who have formed strong bonds of friendship and loyalty with one another, and who will go to great lengths to protect and support their friends and allies.

The main character, Monkey D. Luffy, is a prime example of this theme. Luffy forms a tight-knit group of friends, the Straw Hat Pirates, who share a deep bond of loyalty and trust. Throughout the series, Luffy and his crew demonstrate their loyalty and commitment to one another, often putting their lives on the line to protect their friends and allies.

Additionally, the theme of friendship and loyalty is present in many of the other characters in the series. For example, the relationship between Nami and her adoptive sister Nojiko is a powerful example of the importance of family and loyalty. The two sisters have a strong bond that is rooted in their shared past and their commitment to protecting each other.

The theme of friendship and loyalty also plays a significant role in the series' overarching plot and themes. The main villain of the series, the pirate Blackbeard, represents the opposite of the values of friendship and loyalty. Blackbeard is willing to betray and harm anyone who gets in the way of his ambitions, and his actions demonstrate the destructive nature of greed and selfishness.

The importance of friendship and loyalty in One Piece is a powerful message that resonates with many fans of the series. The bonds formed between characters in the story demonstrate the value of having strong relationships with others, and the lengths that people will go to protect and support their friends and loved ones. This theme adds depth and richness to the series, and helps to make the story and characters relatable and engaging.

THE EVOLUTION OF LUFFY AND HIS CREW'S RELATIONSHIPS

The relationships between the members of the Straw Hat Pirates, Luffy's crew, have evolved significantly throughout the course of One Piece. At the beginning of the series, the crew was made up of a group of individuals who had their own goals and motivations, and who had not yet developed a strong bond of trust and loyalty with one another. However, as the story has progressed, the characters have grown and evolved, and their relationships with one another have become much deeper and more meaningful.

In the early stages of the series, the members of the Straw Hat crew were united by their shared goal of finding the legendary treasure, One Piece. However, as they encountered various challenges and obstacles, they began to rely on one another and develop a sense of trust and camaraderie. For example, in the Arlong Park arc, the crew members united to help Nami free her hometown from the control of the pirate Arlong, demonstrating their loyalty and commitment to one another.

As the series has progressed, the relationships between the characters have become even stronger. For example, the bond between Luffy and his first mate, Zoro, has deepened significantly over the course of the story. Zoro initially joined the crew because he saw potential in Luffy as a leader, but over time, he has come to respect and admire Luffy's strength and determination.

The relationship between Luffy and his navigator, Nami, has also evolved significantly over the course of the story. Initially, Nami was reluctant to join the crew and was primarily interested in using them to achieve her own goals. However, as she has come to know and trust Luffy and the other crew members, she has become much more committed to their shared goal of finding One Piece.

The evolution of the relationships between Luffy and his crew in One Piece is a central part of the series' story and themes. The characters have grown and developed over time, and their relationships with one another have become deeper and more meaningful, demonstrating the power of trust, loyalty, and camaraderie.

THE SIGNIFICANCE OF THE PIRATE KING AND THE ONE PIECE TREASURE

The Pirate King and the One Piece treasure are two of the most significant elements in the world of One Piece, and play a central role in the series' overarching plot and themes.

The Pirate King, Gol D. Roger, was the most notorious and powerful pirate in the world before his execution. He was the only person to have successfully sailed to the end of the Grand Line and discovered the legendary treasure known as One Piece. Roger's final words before his execution sparked a new age of piracy, as he declared that he had left the One Piece treasure in a location where it could be found by anyone who was willing to undertake the dangerous journey to find it.

The One Piece treasure is the ultimate goal of many of the pirate crews in the series, including Luffy and his crew, the Straw Hat Pirates. It is said to contain unimaginable wealth, but it also holds a deeper meaning for those who seek it. For many characters in the series, the One Piece treasure represents the ultimate goal of their lives, and the possibility of achieving their dreams.

The significance of the Pirate King and the One Piece treasure lies in the themes that they represent. The Pirate King represents the idea of achieving one's goals and dreams, even in the face of adversity and opposition. His journey to the end of the Grand Line represents the ultimate challenge, and his success demonstrates that anything is possible with determination and courage.

The One Piece treasure, on the other hand, represents the power of hope and the potential for a brighter future. The idea that anyone can find the treasure and achieve their dreams is a powerful message of hope and inspiration that resonates with many fans of the series.

The significance of the Pirate King and the One Piece treasure in One Piece is a testament to the power of human ambition and the potential for greatness that lies within each of us. The quest for the treasure is a central part of the series' story and themes, and continues to inspire and captivate audiences around the world.

THE LEGACY OF GOL D. ROGER AND THE ROGER PIRATES

Gol D. Roger, the Pirate King, and his crew, the Roger Pirates, have left a lasting legacy in the world of One Piece. Despite being dead for over twenty years, their influence can still be felt in the series through their actions, their accomplishments, and the way that other characters speak about them.

One of the most significant parts of Gol D. Roger's legacy is his reputation as the only person to have successfully sailed to the end of the Grand Line and discovered the One Piece treasure. This feat made him the most notorious and powerful pirate of his time, and his final words before his execution sparked a new age of piracy in the world. The fact that Roger accomplished this incredible feat and achieved his dreams has made him a symbol of inspiration and hope for many of the characters in the series, including the protagonist, Monkey D. Luffy.

In addition to his accomplishments, Roger's personality and character have also left a lasting impact on the series. He was known for his charisma, his sense of humor, and his strong sense of justice, which have inspired many of the characters in the series. His actions and words have continued to motivate and guide other characters, including Luffy, who has vowed to become the Pirate King like Roger.

The legacy of the Roger Pirates is not limited to Gol D. Roger himself. His crew, which included some of the most powerful and skilled pirates in the world, also left their mark on the story. Members of the crew, such as Rayleigh and Shanks, continue to play important roles in the series, and their actions and words have continued to influence the other characters in the story.

The legacy of Gol D. Roger and the Roger Pirates in One Piece is a testament to the power of human ambition and the potential for greatness that lies within each of us. Their accomplishments and personalities have left a lasting impact on the story and the characters, and continue to inspire and captivate audiences around the world.

THE DIFFERENT TYPES OF DEVIL FRUITS IN ONE PIECE: PARAMECIA, ZOAN, AND LOGIA

Devil Fruits are a unique aspect of the world of One Piece, and play a significant role in the series' plot and themes. There are three types of Devil Fruits: Paramecia, Zoan, and Logia, each with their own unique properties and abilities.

Paramecia Devil Fruits are the most common type, and they give the user a wide range of abilities that are not necessarily related to physical transformation. Users of Paramecia fruits can manipulate their bodies in various ways, such as stretching like rubber (as in the case of Luffy) or manipulating their environment with a specific power, like Doflamingo's String-String Fruit.

Zoan Devil Fruits, on the other hand, allow the user to transform into an animal or a hybrid of a human and animal. Zoan users gain increased physical strength and agility in their animal form, but also the limitations that come with being a particular species. The Zoan class is divided into three subcategories: carnivorous, herbivorous, and ancient, each with its own unique set of abilities and powers.

Logia Devil Fruits are the rarest and most powerful type, and they allow the user to transform into a natural element, such as fire or smoke. Logia users can manipulate their element and use it as a weapon, making them incredibly difficult to defeat in battle. They are also able to transform their bodies to avoid physical attacks and have the ability to regenerate from injuries.

The different types of Devil Fruits in One Piece are not only significant for their unique abilities, but also for the way that they reflect the characters who use them. The powers of each fruit are tied to the personality and backstory of the user, and often reflect their desires, motivations, and goals. This adds depth and complexity to the characters, making them more than just simple vessels for superhuman powers.

The different types of Devil Fruits in One Piece are a crucial part of the series' world-building and add an extra layer of depth to the characters and their abilities. Each type of Devil Fruit offers its own unique set of advantages and disadvantages, making the battles in the series all the more thrilling and unpredictable.

THE ROLE OF
THE WORLD GOVERNMENT AND
THE MARINES IN ONE PIECE

The World Government and the Marines are two of the most important institutions in the world of One Piece, and play a central role in the series' plot and themes. The World Government is a global organization that serves as the primary governing body for the world, while the Marines are the World Government's military branch.

The World Government is responsible for maintaining law and order in the world, and is composed of five powerful elders known as the World Nobles, who are protected by the powerful Cipher Pol intelligence agency. The World Government is known for its corruption, and is often portrayed as oppressive and uncaring towards the common people of the world.

The Marines, on the other hand, are the enforcers of the World Government's laws and policies, and are responsible for maintaining order and fighting against piracy. They are organized into various ranks, with the most powerful among them being the Admirals, who are some of the strongest characters in the series.

Throughout the series, the World Government and the Marines are depicted as the primary antagonists, with their actions often opposing the goals and desires of the protagonists, including Monkey D. Luffy and his crew. The World Government's pursuit of power and control over the world is portrayed as a direct threat to the ideals of freedom and individuality that Luffy and his crew represent.

However, the World Government and the Marines are not depicted as completely evil, and some members of these organizations are shown to be honorable and just. This adds complexity to the story and allows for nuanced discussions about power, authority, and governance.

The World Government and the Marines in One Piece play a crucial role in the series' plot and themes, serving as both the primary antagonists and a vehicle for exploring complex political and social issues. Their actions and beliefs are often in direct opposition to those of the protagonists, making for thrilling and engaging conflict throughout the series.

THE HISTORY AND SIGNIFICANCE OF THE ANCIENT WEAPONS

The Ancient Weapons are a crucial aspect of the world of One Piece, and play a significant role in the series' plot and themes. These weapons are powerful and mysterious artifacts that have been hidden away for centuries, and are said to have the ability to destroy entire islands or even the world itself.

There are three known Ancient Weapons: Pluton, Poseidon, and Uranus. Pluton is a powerful battleship that is said to be capable of mass destruction, while Poseidon is a special ability that allows the user to communicate with and control sea kings, massive sea creatures with enormous strength. Uranus, on the other hand, has not yet been fully revealed, but is believed to be another powerful weapon capable of great destruction.

The significance of the Ancient Weapons lies in their connection to the world's history and mythology. The weapons were created during the Void Century, a period of time that is shrouded in mystery and has been intentionally erased from history by the World Government. This has made the weapons highly sought after by various factions and individuals, each with their own motives and goals.

The Ancient Weapons also tie into the themes of power, control, and the consequences of wielding such power. Throughout the series, the characters are forced to confront the possibility of the Ancient Weapons falling into the wrong hands and the devastating consequences that would follow. This raises questions about who should have access to such power and the responsibility that comes with wielding it.

The history and significance of the Ancient Weapons in One Piece are an integral part of the series' world-building and themes. They add an extra layer of depth and complexity to the story, providing a tantalizing mystery that keeps readers and viewers engaged throughout the series.

THE ROLE OF SHICHIBUKAI AND YONKO IN ONE PIECE

The Shichibukai and Yonko are two of the most powerful and influential groups in the world of One Piece. The Shichibukai, also known as the Seven Warlords of the Sea, are a group of seven powerful pirates who have been granted immunity from the World Government in exchange for their services. The Yonko, on the other hand, are a group of four of the most powerful pirate captains in the world.

The Shichibukai and Yonko play a significant role in the power dynamics of the world of One Piece. The Shichibukai act as a balance of power, serving as a check against the other pirate crews and providing a level of stability to the world. The Yonko, on the other hand, are some of the most powerful pirates in the world and control vast territories and resources.

Throughout the series, the Shichibukai and Yonko are often depicted as obstacles to the protagonists' goals. The Shichibukai, despite being technically allied with the World Government, are shown to be opportunistic and often act in their own self-interest. The Yonko, on the other hand, are shown to be ruthless and power-hungry, often engaging in violent conflicts with each other and the World Government.

The role of the Shichibukai and Yonko also ties into the series' themes of power, freedom, and individuality. The Shichibukai and Yonko both represent a certain level of power and freedom that is at odds with the World Government's desire for control and order. This creates a tension between these factions and provides a space for exploring the meaning and value of these concepts.

The Shichibukai and Yonko are crucial elements in the world of One Piece, representing different aspects of power and freedom, and serving as important antagonists and obstacles to the protagonists' goals. Their presence in the series adds an extra layer of complexity and nuance to the story, providing engaging conflicts and exploration of the themes at the heart of the series.

THE SIGNIFICANCE OF THE GRAND LINE AND THE NEW WORLD

In the world of One Piece, the Grand Line and the New World are two of the most significant locations. The Grand Line is a dangerous and unpredictable sea route that encircles the world, while the New World is a region beyond the Grand Line that is even more treacherous and full of powerful pirates and mysterious locations.

The Grand Line is significant because it serves as a central location for the series' overarching story and the journey of the protagonist, Monkey D. Luffy, and his crew. Throughout the series, Luffy and his crew sail through the Grand Line, encountering a wide range of unique islands and strange phenomena, as well as battling powerful opponents. The Grand Line is full of unique features such as the different seasons, magnetic fields, and unpredictable weather patterns that add an extra layer of challenge to the protagonists' journey. Additionally, the Grand Line is home to many ancient and powerful secrets, such as the Poneglyphs and the lost kingdom of Raftel.

The New World, on the other hand, is even more dangerous and mysterious than the Grand Line. It is home to some of the most powerful pirates in the world, such as the Yonko, and features new challenges and obstacles for Luffy and his crew to overcome. The New World is also home to many of the series' most significant locations, such as the island of Dressrosa and the Wano Country.

The significance of the Grand Line and the New World goes beyond the physical locations themselves, however. They represent the idea of the unknown and the importance of exploration and discovery. Luffy and his crew are driven by a desire to explore the world and find the legendary One Piece treasure, which is said to be located at the end of the Grand Line on the fabled island of Raftel. The journey through the Grand Line and the New World is a metaphor for the journey of life and the importance of taking risks and facing challenges to achieve one's goals.

The Grand Line and the New World are significant locations in the world of One Piece, serving as central locations for the series' story and themes, as well as representing the idea of the unknown and the importance of exploration and discovery.

THE SIGNIFICANCE OF THE SUMMIT WAR SAGA AND THE DRESSROSA ARC

The Summit War Saga and the Dressrosa Arc are two of the most significant story arcs in the world of One Piece. The Summit War Saga covers the events leading up to and during the Battle of Marineford, while the Dressrosa Arc features the Straw Hat Pirates' journey to the island of Dressrosa and their battle against the Donquixote Pirates. These two arcs are significant in many ways, including their impact on the series' overarching story and themes.

The Summit War Saga is significant because it marks a turning point in the series, with major revelations and significant character deaths. This arc brings together many of the series' major players, including the Straw Hat Pirates, the Whitebeard Pirates, the Marines, and many other powerful characters. The Battle of Marineford is a major event in the world of One Piece, with the stakes higher than ever before and the consequences of the battle rippling throughout the series.

The Dressrosa Arc is significant for its exploration of themes such as power, corruption, and revolution. The arc features the Straw Hat Pirates' journey to Dressrosa, where they become involved in a conflict between the Donquixote Pirates and the citizens of the island. This arc introduces new characters, including the powerful Donquixote family and the revolutionary Sabo, and features significant character development for many of the series' central characters. The arc also sets up the events leading into the later arcs of the series, with many of the themes explored in Dressrosa continuing to play a significant role in the series.

the Summit War Saga and the Dressrosa Arc are significant story arcs in the world of One Piece. They explore important themes and advance the series' overarching story, while also introducing new characters and setting up the events of future arcs. These two arcs are prime examples of the depth and complexity of the world of One Piece and are essential viewing for any fan of the series.

THE IMPORTANCE OF DREAMS AND ASPIRATIONS IN ONE PIECE

One Piece is a story about dreams and aspirations. The central character, Monkey D. Luffy, is driven by a powerful desire to become the Pirate King, and he gathers a crew of like-minded individuals who each have their own dreams and goals. Throughout the series, the importance of dreams and aspirations is a recurring theme, with the characters fighting to achieve their goals in the face of adversity and opposition.

One of the key aspects of the importance of dreams in One Piece is the idea that everyone has the right to pursue their own dreams, regardless of the circumstances of their birth or the obstacles they face. The series emphasizes the idea that anyone can achieve their dreams if they work hard enough and are determined to succeed. This is exemplified by Luffy and his crew, who come from humble beginnings but are driven by their dreams to achieve great things.

The series also explores the idea that having a dream or aspiration can give people a sense of purpose and direction in life. The characters in One Piece are motivated by their dreams, and their pursuit of those dreams gives their lives meaning and significance. This is particularly evident in the character of Chopper, a reindeer who dreamed of becoming a doctor and who joins Luffy's crew to pursue that dream. For Chopper, his dream is not just a goal to strive for but a defining part of his identity.

Finally, the importance of dreams and aspirations in One Piece is also tied to the idea of freedom. The series emphasizes the idea that achieving one's dreams is a way to achieve true freedom, both from external constraints and from internal limitations. Luffy and his crew are driven by a desire to live their lives on their own terms, and the pursuit of their dreams is a way to make that a reality.

The importance of dreams and aspirations is a central theme in One Piece. The series emphasizes the idea that pursuing one's dreams is a fundamental right and a source of purpose and meaning in life. This theme adds depth and resonance to the series and helps to make it a powerful and inspiring story.

THE SIGNIFICANCE OF THE STRAW HAT PIRATES AND THEIR ALLIES

The Straw Hat Pirates are the central characters of the One Piece series, and they are a highly significant group within the story. Led by Monkey D. Luffy, the Straw Hat Pirates are a group of pirate adventurers who sail the Grand Line in search of the legendary treasure known as One Piece. Throughout their adventures, they encounter numerous allies and enemies, and their relationships with these characters are an important part of the series.

One of the key significances of the Straw Hat Pirates and their allies is the way in which they demonstrate the power of teamwork and friendship. The series emphasizes the idea that the Straw Hat Pirates are stronger together than they are apart, and that their bonds of friendship and loyalty are what enable them to overcome even the most difficult challenges. This is exemplified by the crew's determination to rescue their crewmate, Nico Robin, during the Enies Lobby arc, as well as their willingness to sacrifice themselves for each other during the Marineford War.

Another significance of the Straw Hat Pirates and their allies is the way in which they represent a diverse range of personalities and backgrounds. Each member of the crew has their own unique strengths and weaknesses, and their different perspectives and approaches to problem-solving are a key part of their success. Additionally, the crew's allies come from a wide range of backgrounds, including pirates, revolutionaries, and even former enemies. This diversity of perspectives and experiences adds depth and complexity to the story, and helps to create a rich and nuanced world.

Finally, the Straw Hat Pirates and their allies are significant because of the way in which they challenge the status quo and fight against injustice. The crew is often at odds with the World Government and the Marine forces, and they are driven by a desire to create a world in which people can pursue their dreams and live freely.

Additionally, the crew's allies include individuals who are fighting against oppressive regimes and who are seeking to create a better world. Through their actions, the Straw Hat Pirates and their allies demonstrate the power of standing up for what is right and fighting for a better future.

The Straw Hat Pirates and their allies are highly significant within the One Piece series. They represent the power of teamwork and friendship, the importance of diversity and different perspectives, and the value of standing up against injustice. Their relationships with each other and with other characters add depth and richness to the story, and make One Piece a compelling and inspiring series.

THE IMPORTANCE OF ONE PIECE'S THEMES: FREEDOM, JUSTICE, AND ADVENTURE

One Piece is a series that is rich with themes that explore some of the most fundamental and universal aspects of the human experience. Three of the most important themes in the series are freedom, justice, and adventure. These themes are not only central to the story and the characters, but they also resonate with audiences around the world.

The theme of freedom is a key aspect of One Piece. Throughout the series, the characters are driven by a desire to be free from oppression and to live their lives on their own terms. This is exemplified by the Straw Hat Pirates, who reject the idea of being ruled by others and who are constantly seeking to break free from the constraints of the world around them. The theme of freedom is also closely tied to the idea of individualism, and the series celebrates the idea of people pursuing their dreams and following their own paths in life.

The theme of justice is another important aspect of One Piece. The series explores the idea of what it means to be just and to fight for what is right.

This is exemplified by the Marine forces, who are tasked with maintaining law and order in the world, but who are also depicted as being flawed and corrupt at times. The characters in the series are often driven by a desire to see justice done, and they are willing to fight for what they believe in, even if it means going against the established order.

Finally, the theme of adventure is a central part of One Piece. The series celebrates the idea of exploration and discovery, and the characters are constantly on the move, seeking out new experiences and challenges. This theme is closely tied to the idea of personal growth and development, as the characters are often forced to confront their own limitations and to overcome obstacles in order to achieve their goals.

Taken together, the themes of freedom, justice, and adventure are an integral part of what makes One Piece such a beloved and enduring series. These themes resonate with audiences around the world, and they speak to some of the most fundamental aspects of the human experience. Through its exploration of these themes, One Piece offers a powerful message of hope and inspiration, reminding us of the importance of fighting for what we believe in and of living life on our own terms.

THE LEGACY OF ONE PIECE: LOOKING BACK AND LOOKING FORWARD

As one of the most popular and influential anime and manga series of all time, One Piece has left an indelible mark on popular culture and continues to inspire fans around the world. With over 1,000 chapters of the manga and more than 900 episodes of the anime, the series has created a vast and richly detailed world that is both complex and engaging.

One of the key factors in the enduring popularity of One Piece is its ability to appeal to a wide range of audiences. The series has something for everyone, from action-packed battles and epic adventure to complex character development and emotional storytelling. It also addresses important themes such as freedom, justice, and loyalty, making it a series that is both entertaining and thought-provoking.

Looking back at the legacy of One Piece, it is clear that the series has had a profound impact on the anime and manga industry.

The success of the series has paved the way for other long-running shonen anime and manga, and its influence can be seen in countless other works in the genre. The characters and themes of One Piece have also become iconic, inspiring countless fan art, cosplay, and merchandise.

Looking forward, the legacy of One Piece seems set to continue. The series is still ongoing, and fans are eagerly anticipating the conclusion of the story. The creator of the series, Eiichiro Oda, has stated that the series is approximately 80% complete, and it is clear that he has a clear vision for the story's endgame. With the conclusion of the manga on the horizon, it seems likely that the legacy of One Piece will continue to grow and evolve for years to come.

The legacy of One Piece is a testament to the power of storytelling and the enduring appeal of well-crafted characters and themes. As fans continue to enjoy the adventures of the Straw Hat Pirates, it is clear that the series will continue to inspire and entertain audiences around the world for years to come.

THE ROLE OF SEA KINGS AND SEA MONSTERS IN ONE PIECE

One Piece is a popular Japanese manga and anime series that revolves around the adventures of Monkey D. Luffy, a young pirate who sets out to find the legendary treasure known as the One Piece and become the King of the Pirates. Throughout his journey, Luffy and his crew encounter various sea kings and sea monsters, which play an important role in the story.

Sea kings are enormous sea creatures that inhabit the oceans of the One Piece world. They are said to be the guardians of the sea and are respected by pirates and marine soldiers alike. In the series, sea kings are depicted as intelligent beings that possess the ability to communicate with humans. They are often seen helping the protagonists in their quest or warning them of impending danger.

One of the most notable sea kings in the series is the Sea King that swallowed Luffy's brother, Portgas D. Ace. This Sea King, also known as the "Lord of the Coast," is the first sea king that Luffy encounters in the series. Despite being an antagonist at first, the Lord of the Coast later becomes a recurring ally to Luffy and his crew.

Another sea king that plays a significant role in the series is the Kraken. The Kraken is a massive sea monster that resides in the deep sea and is known for its destructive power. It is first introduced in the series as an antagonist that attacks the Thousand Sunny, Luffy's ship. However, the Kraken later becomes a valuable ally to Luffy and his crew, aiding them in their battle against the World Government.

Sea monsters, on the other hand, are creatures that are not necessarily intelligent but are still a formidable threat to those who travel the seas. In One Piece, sea monsters come in various shapes and sizes, from giant squids to massive sea serpents. They are often depicted as creatures that attack ships and devour their crew.

One of the most prominent sea monsters in the series is the giant sea serpent known as the Sea King. The Sea King is a massive creature that is feared by many sailors and pirates alike. It is first introduced in the series as an antagonist that attacks Luffy's crew, but later becomes a recurring ally to the protagonists.

Another sea monster that plays an important role in the series is the Kraken, which is also considered a sea monster in addition to being a sea king. The Kraken is a massive creature that is feared by many pirates and is known for its destructive power. It is first introduced in the series as an antagonist that attacks Luffy's ship, but later becomes a valuable ally to the protagonists.

Sea kings and sea monsters play a significant role in the One Piece series. They are often depicted as intelligent beings that possess the ability to communicate with humans and are respected by pirates and marine soldiers alike. Sea monsters, on the other hand, are creatures that are not necessarily intelligent but are still a formidable threat to those who travel the seas. Despite their differences, both sea kings and sea monsters serve as important obstacles for the protagonists to overcome in their quest for the One Piece.

THE SIGNIFICANCE OF THE MARINEFORD WAR AND ITS AFTERMATH

The Marineford War is one of the most significant events in the One Piece series. It is a battle that takes place in Marineford, the headquarters of the World Government, and involves several powerful characters from the series. The war has far-reaching consequences and shapes the direction of the story going forward.

The Marineford War is significant for several reasons. Firstly, it is the first time that the protagonist, Monkey D. Luffy, directly challenges the World Government. Luffy and his crew enter Marineford to rescue his brother, Portgas D. Ace, who is being held captive and sentenced to execution by the World Government. The war marks a turning point in Luffy's journey, as he begins to move from being a simple pirate to becoming a major threat to the World Government.

Secondly, the Marineford War brings together several powerful characters from the One Piece series, including many of the Seven Warlords of the Sea, powerful pirates who have allied themselves with the World Government in exchange for certain privileges. The war also involves several high-ranking members of the Marines, including Admiral Akainu, Admiral Aokiji, and Admiral Kizaru. The presence of so many powerful characters in one place makes the Marineford War an epic battle and a memorable moment in the series.

Thirdly, the Marineford War has significant consequences for the story going forward. The war leads to the death of Portgas D. Ace, Luffy's brother, which has a profound impact on Luffy's character and motivates him to become stronger and to pursue his dream of becoming the Pirate King. The war also leads to the resignation of several high-ranking members of the Marines, including Admiral Aokiji, who leaves the organization due to disagreements with the new direction it is taking under the leadership of Admiral Akainu.

Furthermore, the aftermath of the Marineford War has significant consequences for the world of One Piece. The war leads to a shift in the balance of power, as several powerful characters are eliminated or weakened. The World Government is also forced to acknowledge the growing threat posed by Luffy and his allies and begins to take more aggressive measures to suppress their activities. The war also leads to the introduction of several new characters, including the mysterious figure known as "Blackbeard," who emerges as a major player in the world of One Piece following the war.

The Marineford War is a significant event in the One Piece series, both for its epic battles and its far-reaching consequences. The war marks a turning point in the story, as Luffy and his crew begin to move from being simple pirates to becoming major threats to the World Government. The war also brings together several powerful characters from the series and has significant consequences for the story going forward. the Marineford War is a memorable moment in the One Piece series that continues to shape the direction of the story today.

THE EVOLUTION OF
ONE PIECE'S VILLAINS:
FROM ARLONG TO BLACKBEARD

One Piece is a story filled with memorable characters, and perhaps none more so than the series' villains. From Arlong to Blackbeard, the evolution of One Piece's villains has been a key part of the series' success.

Arlong, the series' first major villain, is a fish-man pirate who seeks to dominate the East Blue, a region of the One Piece world. Arlong is a brutal and ruthless character, willing to do whatever it takes to achieve his goals. He is also one of the series' most memorable villains, with a distinctive design and a menacing presence.

As the series progresses, the villains become increasingly complex and multifaceted. Crocodile, the villain of the Alabasta arc, is a shrewd and calculating character who uses his position as a Warlord of the Sea to manipulate the government and control the region of Alabasta. He is a formidable opponent for Luffy and his crew, and his defeat marks a major turning point in the series.

Enel, the villain of the Skypiea arc, is perhaps the most powerful villain Luffy and his crew have faced up to that point in the series. Enel is a god-like figure who controls lightning and is worshipped by the inhabitants of Skypiea. He is a deeply arrogant character who views himself as invincible, and his eventual defeat by Luffy is a satisfying moment for readers.

As the series progresses, the villains become more nuanced and complex. Rob Lucci, the villain of the Enies Lobby arc, is a member of the World Government's secret intelligence agency, Cipher Pol 9. He is a cold and calculating character who is willing to sacrifice anything and anyone to achieve his goals. However, he also has a tragic backstory, which makes his defeat at the hands of Luffy and his crew all the more satisfying.

Blackbeard, the series' most recent major villain, is a complex and multifaceted character who represents a significant challenge for Luffy and his crew. Blackbeard is a former member of Whitebeard's crew, and his actions throughout the series suggest that he is driven by a deep sense of ambition and a desire for power. He is also a cunning and intelligent character, with a deep understanding of the world of One Piece and the people who inhabit it.

The evolution of One Piece's villains has been a key part of the series' success. From the brutish Arlong to the complex and multifaceted Blackbeard, the villains of One Piece have been memorable and engaging characters who have provided a significant challenge for Luffy and his crew. As the series continues to progress, it will be interesting to see how the villains evolve and how they continue to shape the direction of the story.

THE DIFFERENT TYPES OF HAKI: OBSERVATION, ARMAMENT, AND CONQUEROR'S

In the world of One Piece, Haki is a powerful ability that allows its users to tap into their spiritual energy and achieve a range of incredible feats. There are three different types of Haki: Observation Haki, Armament Haki, and Conqueror's Haki. Each type of Haki has its own unique abilities and uses, and mastering them is a key part of becoming a powerful fighter in the One Piece world.

Observation Haki, also known as Kenbunshoku Haki, is the ability to sense the presence of others and predict their movements. Those who are proficient in this type of Haki can detect the emotions and intentions of those around them, and can even sense attacks before they happen. This ability is particularly useful in combat, allowing its users to dodge attacks and counter their opponents with great precision.

Armament Haki, also known as Busoshoku Haki, is the ability to harden one's own body or objects with one's own Haki. This ability allows its users to imbue their attacks with incredible strength and durability, and is particularly useful for defeating opponents who possess strong physical defenses. This ability can also be used to protect oneself from harm, allowing its users to withstand powerful attacks that would otherwise be fatal.

Conqueror's Haki, also known as Haoshoku Haki, is the rarest and most powerful type of Haki. Those who possess this ability have the power to intimidate and overpower others with their sheer willpower. This ability allows its users to dominate weak-willed individuals and even knock them unconscious. It is a highly sought-after ability in the One Piece world, and only a select few individuals have been shown to possess it.

Mastering Haki is a key part of becoming a powerful fighter in the One Piece world. Each type of Haki has its own unique abilities and uses, and mastering all three is essential for those who seek to become the strongest fighters in the world. However, Haki is not just about physical strength; it is also a reflection of one's mental and emotional state. Those who possess strong willpower and a clear sense of purpose are more likely to master Haki than those who lack these qualities.

The different types of Haki in One Piece provide a rich and complex system of abilities and powers that add depth and complexity to the series. Observation Haki, Armament Haki, and Conqueror's Haki each have their own unique strengths and weaknesses, and mastering them is essential for any fighter who hopes to succeed in the world of One Piece. As the series continues to progress, it will be interesting to see how Haki continues to evolve and how it will continue to shape the direction of the story.

THE SIGNIFICANCE OF THE WORLD NOBLES AND THE SABAODY ARCHIPELAGO

In the world of One Piece, the World Nobles are a powerful and influential group of individuals who are considered to be above the law. They are descended from the founding families of the World Government and possess immense wealth and influence. The Sabaody Archipelago, located in the New World, is a key location in the story of One Piece and plays a significant role in the narrative surrounding the World Nobles.

The World Nobles are feared and revered throughout the One Piece world, and their mere presence is enough to send most people running in fear. They are protected by an army of highly trained soldiers known as the Marines, and any attempt to harm them is met with swift and brutal punishment. Despite their immense power and wealth, however, the World Nobles are also deeply hated by many people throughout the world, who view them as corrupt and evil.

The Sabaody Archipelago is a hub of activity for pirates and traders alike, and is also home to the infamous Human Auctioning House, where slaves are bought and sold like commodities. It is here that the Straw Hat Pirates first encounter the World Nobles, and the events that transpire on Sabaody Archipelago set the stage for many of the major plot points in the series.

The significance of the World Nobles and the Sabaody Archipelago lies in the way they highlight the injustices and inequalities that exist in the One Piece world. The World Nobles are a symbol of the corrupt and oppressive nature of the World Government, and their treatment of ordinary people is a testament to the cruelty and callousness of those in power.

The events that unfold on Sabaody Archipelago highlight the stark contrast between the rich and powerful and the poor and oppressed. The Straw Hat Pirates, who are themselves outsiders and outcasts, are appalled by the treatment of the slaves and are determined to do something about it. Their actions on Sabaody Archipelago serve as a reminder that even in a world where power and wealth are concentrated in the hands of a few, there are still those who are willing to stand up for what is right.

In addition to its social commentary, the Sabaody Archipelago arc also plays a key role in the overall narrative of One Piece. The events that unfold here set the stage for the Marineford War, which is one of the most significant and impactful events in the entire series. The discovery of the ancient weapon known as the Thousand Sunny, which takes place on Sabaody Archipelago, also serves as a major plot point in the series.

The significance of the World Nobles and the Sabaody Archipelago lies in their ability to highlight the injustices and inequalities that exist in the One Piece world, and their role in setting the stage for some of the most significant events in the series. Through its exploration of these themes, One Piece offers a thought-provoking and engaging commentary on power, wealth, and the human condition.

THE ROLE OF THE REVOLUTIONARY ARMY AND ITS LEADERS

In the world of One Piece, the Revolutionary Army is a powerful organization that seeks to overthrow the corrupt World Government and bring about a new era of freedom and equality. Led by the enigmatic and charismatic Monkey D. Dragon, the Revolutionary Army is a key player in the ongoing struggle for power and control in the One Piece world.

The role of the Revolutionary Army is multifaceted, with their actions ranging from covert operations to full-scale battles. They operate in secret, working behind the scenes to gather information and plan their next move. Their ultimate goal is to bring down the World Government, which they view as a corrupt and oppressive institution that is responsible for the suffering and misery of countless people throughout the world.

At the head of the Revolutionary Army is Monkey D. Dragon, a man of mystery and intrigue. Little is known about his past or his motivations, but it is clear that he is a charismatic leader who commands the loyalty and respect of his followers. He is also the father of Monkey D. Luffy, the protagonist of the series, which adds an additional layer of complexity to his character and his relationship with the other characters in the series.

Other key members of the Revolutionary Army include Sabo, a childhood friend of Luffy's who was presumed dead until he resurfaced as a member of the organization, and Koala, a former slave who was rescued by the Revolutionary Army and now works as a spy and operative for the organization. These characters, along with others, add depth and nuance to the Revolutionary Army and help to flesh out the organization as a whole.

The role of the Revolutionary Army is significant in the overall narrative of One Piece. Their struggle against the World Government serves as a reminder of the ongoing fight for freedom and equality, and their actions have a profound impact on the world around them. Their influence is felt in everything from political maneuvering to all-out battles, and their presence is a constant reminder that the world of One Piece is one in which power and control are constantly being contested.

In addition to their role in the ongoing narrative of One Piece, the Revolutionary Army also serves as a symbol of hope and inspiration for the other characters in the series. Their commitment to justice and their willingness to fight against oppression and tyranny serves as a beacon of light in a world that is often dark and cruel. They are a reminder that even in the face of overwhelming odds, it is possible to stand up for what is right and fight for a better future.

The role of the Revolutionary Army and its leaders in One Piece is significant and multifaceted. Through their actions and their beliefs, they serve as a powerful symbol of hope and inspiration for the other characters in the series, and their struggle against the World Government adds depth and complexity to the ongoing narrative of the series. Whether operating in secret or engaging in all-out battle, the Revolutionary Army remains a key player in the ongoing struggle for power and control in the world of One Piece.

THE SIGNIFICANCE OF THE VOID CENTURY AND THE ANCIENT KINGDOM

The Void Century is a period of time in the history of the One Piece world that remains shrouded in mystery and intrigue. Very little is known about this era, but what is clear is that it holds significant importance for the overall narrative of the series. The significance of the Void Century lies in its connection to the Ancient Kingdom, a powerful civilization that existed long ago and whose legacy continues to shape the world of One Piece to this day.

According to the lore of One Piece, the Ancient Kingdom was a powerful civilization that existed during the Void Century. This kingdom possessed advanced technology and knowledge that far exceeded that of any other civilization at the time. However, the exact nature of this knowledge and technology remains unknown, as the World Government, which was founded in the aftermath of the Void Century, has worked tirelessly to suppress information about this era.

The significance of the Ancient Kingdom lies in the fact that it was a symbol of hope and freedom in a world that was beset by chaos and conflict. The people of the Ancient Kingdom believed in the importance of individual freedom and the inherent worth of all people, regardless of their race or social status. They also possessed an advanced understanding of the power of the ancient weapons, three powerful artifacts that were said to be capable of destroying entire islands.

The downfall of the Ancient Kingdom came at the hands of the World Government, a powerful institution that was founded in the aftermath of the Void Century. The World Government believed in the importance of control and order, and they saw the Ancient Kingdom as a threat to their vision of a stable and secure world. The exact nature of the conflict between the two civilizations remains unknown, but it is clear that the World Government emerged victorious, and the legacy of the Ancient Kingdom was all but erased from history.

Despite the efforts of the World Government to suppress information about the Void Century and the Ancient Kingdom, fragments of the truth have managed to survive. The Poneglyphs, ancient stone tablets that contain information about the Void Century and the ancient weapons, are scattered throughout the One Piece world, and those who are able to decipher their meaning are able to piece together a more complete picture of this era.

The significance of the Void Century and the Ancient Kingdom lies in the fact that they represent a time of great conflict and upheaval in the history of the One Piece world. They also serve as a reminder of the ongoing struggle for power and control in this world, as well as the importance of individual freedom and the inherent worth of all people.

The significance of the Void Century and the Ancient Kingdom in One Piece cannot be overstated. These two concepts are integral to the overall narrative of the series, and they serve as a reminder of the ongoing struggle for power and control in the world of One Piece. As the story of One Piece continues to unfold, it is likely that more information about the Void Century and the Ancient Kingdom will be revealed, adding depth and complexity to this already rich and compelling world.

THE EVOLUTION OF ONE PIECE'S FEMALE CHARACTERS: FROM NAMI TO BOA HANCOCK

One Piece is a popular anime and manga series that has been praised for its intricate plot, well-developed characters, and unique world-building. One aspect of the series that has been the focus of much discussion is the evolution of its female characters. Over the course of the series, One Piece's female characters have undergone significant changes, both in terms of their appearance and their characterization. From Nami to Boa Hancock, the female characters in One Piece have become more complex and dynamic, reflecting the series' commitment to exploring a wide range of human experiences.

Nami, one of the first female characters introduced in the series, was initially portrayed as a damsel in distress. Her primary function was to provide support for the male characters and to be rescued when necessary. However, as the series progressed, Nami became more assertive and independent, demonstrating her own skills and abilities. She also became a more complex character, with her own motivations and desires.

Similarly, Robin, another early female character in One Piece, started out as a mysterious and enigmatic figure. Her initial role was to provide exposition about the world of One Piece and to assist the Straw Hat crew in their adventures. However, as the series progressed, Robin's character became more fleshed out, and her tragic backstory was revealed. She became a more active participant in the story, using her intelligence and knowledge to help the Straw Hat crew in their battles.

The introduction of new female characters, such as Vivi and Rebecca, continued this trend of portraying women as complex and multifaceted individuals. Vivi, in particular, was a notable departure from the typical female character archetype in shonen anime and manga. She was not a fighter, but rather a diplomat and a strategist, and her intelligence and resourcefulness were key to the success of the Straw Hat crew.

Boa Hancock, one of the most popular female characters in the series, represents the culmination of this evolution. She is a powerful warrior who commands respect and admiration from those around her. Her beauty and charm are a major part of her character, but she is also fiercely independent and determined to achieve her own goals. Her past trauma and struggles have also been explored, adding depth and complexity to her character.

One aspect of the evolution of One Piece's female characters that has been particularly noteworthy is the way in which their appearances have changed. Early in the series, female characters were often sexualized and objectified, with exaggerated curves and revealing outfits. However, as the series has progressed, the female characters have been depicted in a more realistic and less sexualized manner. This reflects a growing awareness in the anime and manga industry of the harmful effects of objectification and the importance of portraying women as individuals rather than mere objects of desire.

The evolution of One Piece's female characters has been a positive development for the series. By portraying women as complex and multifaceted individuals, the series has been able to explore a wide range of human experiences and emotions. This has helped to make the world of One Piece more rich and compelling, and has attracted a wider audience to the series. As the series continues, it will be interesting to see how the female characters continue to evolve and grow, and how their experiences will continue to shape the story of One Piece.

THE ROLE OF THE SUPERNOVAS AND THEIR CONTRIBUTIONS TO ONE PIECE

The Supernovas are a group of powerful and influential pirates in the world of One Piece. They are a collection of rookie pirates who were all introduced during the Sabaody Archipelago arc. Each of them has a bounty of at least 100 million berries, which is an impressive feat for pirates who are just starting out on their careers. Over the course of the series, the Supernovas have become an important part of the world of One Piece, and their contributions to the story have been significant.

One of the main roles of the Supernovas in One Piece is to provide a counterbalance to the Yonko, the four most powerful pirate captains in the world. The Yonko are the dominant force in the New World, and they hold immense power and influence. However, the arrival of the Supernovas has upset this balance, and they have become a force to be reckoned with. By challenging the Yonko, the Supernovas have introduced a new dynamic into the world of One Piece, and they have forced the established power structures to adapt and change.

Another important role of the Supernovas is to provide a source of conflict and tension in the story. Each of the Supernovas has their own goals and motivations, and they are not always aligned with each other. This has led to a number of interesting and complex relationships between the different members of the group. For example, Kid and Law have a tense and adversarial relationship, while Luffy and Law have become close allies. These relationships have provided a rich source of drama and tension in the story, and they have helped to keep the audience engaged and invested in the series.

In addition to their roles as challengers to the established power structures and sources of conflict, the Supernovas have also made significant contributions to the story in other ways. For example, they have introduced a number of new Devil Fruit powers into the series, such as Eustass Kid's Magnet-Magnet Fruit and Jewelry Bonney's Time-Time Fruit. These powers have added new dimensions to the battles in One Piece, and they have made the fights more dynamic and exciting.

The Supernovas have also provided a number of interesting and complex characterizations. Each of the Supernovas has their own unique personality and backstory, and they have been fleshed out over the course of the series. For example, Law's tragic past and his motivations for taking down the Yonko have been explored in great detail, while Kid's ruthless and violent nature has been contrasted with Luffy's more compassionate and carefree outlook.

The Supernovas have been a significant and important part of the world of One Piece. They have challenged the established power structures, provided a source of conflict and tension, introduced new Devil Fruit powers, and added depth and complexity to the characters in the series. As the story continues to unfold, it will be interesting to see how the role of the Supernovas evolves, and how they will continue to shape the world of One Piece.

THE SIGNIFICANCE OF RAFTEL AND THE ONE PIECE TREASURE

Raftel is an island that is said to be the final destination of the Grand Line, the most dangerous and challenging sea route in the world of One Piece. It is also the place where the legendary treasure known as One Piece is said to be located. The significance of Raftel and the One Piece treasure is a major driving force in the story of One Piece, and it has captivated the imagination of fans since the beginning of the series.

One of the key reasons why Raftel and the One Piece treasure are so significant is that they represent the ultimate goal of the main character, Monkey D. Luffy, and his crew, the Straw Hat Pirates. Luffy's dream is to become the Pirate King, the most powerful and respected pirate in the world. To achieve this goal, he needs to find One Piece, and to do that, he needs to reach Raftel. This journey has been the central focus of the story, and it has led Luffy and his crew on a series of adventures across the world of One Piece.

Another reason why Raftel and the One Piece treasure are significant is that they are shrouded in mystery and intrigue. Very little is known about either of them, and the few hints that have been dropped throughout the series have only served to heighten the sense of mystery and anticipation. Fans have speculated for years about what the One Piece treasure might be, and what secrets Raftel might hold. This has created a sense of excitement and anticipation that has kept fans engaged with the series.

In addition to being the ultimate goal of Luffy and his crew, Raftel and the One Piece treasure also represent the culmination of the overarching themes and messages of One Piece. One Piece is a series that is deeply concerned with issues of freedom, justice, and the pursuit of one's dreams. The idea of One Piece as a treasure that can only be found by those who have the courage and determination to pursue their dreams to the end embodies these themes perfectly. It is a message that has resonated with fans all over the world, and it has helped to make One Piece one of the most popular and beloved anime and manga series of all time.

Finally, the significance of Raftel and the One Piece treasure lies in the fact that they represent the end of the story. One Piece has been running for over two decades, and it is one of the longest and most successful anime and manga series in history. However, it is also a series that has a clear endpoint in mind. The journey to Raftel and the discovery of One Piece will mark the end of the story of Luffy and his crew, and it will be a moment that fans have been waiting for since the beginning. This final reveal is sure to be one of the most anticipated and celebrated moments in anime and manga history.

The significance of Raftel and the One Piece treasure in the world of One Piece cannot be overstated. They represent the ultimate goal of the main character and his crew, they are shrouded in mystery and intrigue, they embody the overarching themes and messages of the series, and they mark the end of one of the most popular and beloved anime and manga series of all time. The journey to Raftel and the discovery of One Piece has been the driving force of the series since its inception, and it will be a moment that fans will never forget.

THE EVOLUTION OF THE STRAW HAT PIRATES' BOUNTIES AND NOTORIETY

The Straw Hat Pirates are one of the most notorious pirate crews in the world of One Piece, and their reputation and bounties have evolved significantly over the course of the series. From their humble beginnings as a small group of friends seeking adventure and freedom, they have become one of the most feared and respected pirate crews in the world, with bounties that reflect their growing notoriety and power.

At the start of the series, the Straw Hats had no bounties, and they were relatively unknown in the world of One Piece. However, as they began to make a name for themselves through their adventures and battles, their bounties started to increase. The first member of the crew to receive a bounty was Monkey D. Luffy, the captain, who was given a bounty of 30 million berries after defeating the powerful pirate Don Krieg. From there, the bounties of the other crew members began to rise as well, reflecting their growing reputation and power.

As the Straw Hats became more notorious, their bounties became increasingly significant. Luffy's bounty, in particular, has increased dramatically over the course of the series, from 30 million berries to 1.5 billion berries by the most recent chapter. This increase in bounty reflects Luffy's growing strength and influence, as well as his reputation as one of the most dangerous pirates in the world.

In addition to their bounties, the Straw Hats' notoriety has also evolved over the course of the series. At the start, they were seen as a relatively harmless group of adventurers, but as they became more powerful and influential, they began to attract the attention of some of the most powerful forces in the world, including the World Government and the Four Emperors. Their actions have had a significant impact on the world of One Piece, and they have become a symbol of rebellion and defiance against the established order.

The evolution of the Straw Hats' bounties and notoriety has had a significant impact on the story of One Piece. As their bounties have increased, they have become the targets of more powerful enemies, and they have been forced to fight harder and more strategically to survive. At the same time, their growing notoriety has made them more influential and respected among other pirate crews, and they have become key players in the battle for control of the world.

One of the most significant moments in the evolution of the Straw Hats' bounties and notoriety was the events of the Dressrosa arc. In this arc, the Straw Hats were instrumental in overthrowing a corrupt ruler and restoring order to a troubled kingdom. As a result of their actions, their bounties increased significantly, and they became known as the "heroes of Dressrosa." This event marked a turning point in the story of One Piece, as it demonstrated the impact that the Straw Hats could have on the world and their growing influence on the events that were unfolding.

The evolution of the Straw Hats' bounties and notoriety is a key aspect of the story of One Piece. It reflects their growing reputation and power, as well as the impact that they have had on the world of One Piece. As their bounties have increased and their notoriety has grown, they have become key players in the battle for control of the world, and their actions have had a significant impact on the course of the story. The evolution of their bounties and notoriety is a testament to their strength, determination, and the impact that they have had on the world of One Piece.

THE DIFFERENT TYPES OF WEAPONS AND THEIR SIGNIFICANCE IN ONE PIECE

Weapons play a significant role in the world of One Piece, as they are often used in battles between pirates, marines, and other powerful forces. There are many different types of weapons in One Piece, each with their own unique properties and significance.

One of the most common types of weapons in One Piece is the sword. Swords are used by many characters in the series, including some of the most powerful fighters. The swords in One Piece are often imbued with special powers, such as the ability to cut through any substance or the ability to create powerful shockwaves. One of the most significant swords in the series is the legendary sword, known as the "Meito," which is said to be one of the 12 greatest swords in the world.

Another type of weapon in One Piece is the gun. Guns are often used by marines and other military forces, and they are particularly effective against opponents who rely on close-range combat. Some of the guns in One Piece are also imbued with special powers, such as the ability to fire bullets that explode on impact.

In addition to swords and guns, there are also many other types of weapons in One Piece, including axes, spears, and even musical instruments. Each of these weapons has its own unique properties and significance, and they are often used by characters who have specialized skills or fighting styles.

One of the most significant aspects of weapons in One Piece is their connection to the concept of "Haki." Haki is a special ability that allows characters to sense and manipulate the emotions and willpower of others. There are three types of Haki in One Piece: Observation Haki, which allows characters to sense the presence of others; Armament Haki, which allows characters to harden their bodies and weapons; and Conqueror's Haki, which allows characters to overpower weaker opponents and even damage their surroundings.

Weapons play a significant role in the use and development of Haki in One Piece. For example, characters who use swords often develop strong Observation Haki, as they must be able to sense the movements and intentions of their opponents in order to strike with precision. Similarly, characters who use guns often develop strong Armament Haki, as they must be able to create bullets that can penetrate even the toughest defenses.

Another significant aspect of weapons in One Piece is their connection to the history and lore of the world. Many of the most powerful weapons in One Piece are imbued with special powers that are tied to ancient legends and myths. For example, the ancient weapon "Pluton" is said to have the power to destroy entire islands, and its existence is shrouded in mystery and legend.

Weapons play a significant role in the world of One Piece, both in terms of their significance in battle and their connection to the lore and history of the world. Swords, guns, and other types of weapons are used by many characters in the series, and each type of weapon has its own unique properties and significance. The connection between weapons and Haki also adds a deeper layer of significance to the role of weapons in One Piece, as they are often used as tools to develop and strengthen the abilities of the characters who wield them.

THE ROLE OF THE LOG POSE AND THE NEW WORLD NAVIGATION

The Log Pose is a navigational tool used in the world of One Piece that plays a crucial role in the story. It allows characters to navigate through the unpredictable and dangerous seas of the New World, and is essential for any pirate crew that hopes to find the legendary treasure known as One Piece.

The Log Pose is a special compass that points towards islands with magnetic fields that are unique to the New World. These islands are known as "islands of magnetic rock," and they are impossible to navigate to without the use of a Log Pose. Once a Log Pose is set to a particular island, it takes a specific amount of time for it to fully "lock on" to the magnetic field of that island. The length of time it takes for the Log Pose to lock on to an island varies, and can range from a few hours to several days.

The Log Pose is a critical tool for any pirate crew that hopes to navigate through the treacherous waters of the New World. The New World is full of dangerous sea creatures, unpredictable weather patterns, and dangerous pirate crews. Without the use of a Log Pose, a crew could easily become lost in the vast and unpredictable seas of the New World, putting themselves and their ship at risk.

The Log Pose also plays a significant role in the overall story of One Piece. The concept of the Log Pose is closely tied to the idea of exploration and discovery, which is a major theme throughout the series. The Log Pose represents the challenge of navigating through the unknown and the rewards that come with the discovery of new islands, new treasures, and new allies.

The Log Pose is not without its limitations, however. It is entirely reliant on the magnetic fields of the islands it points to, which can sometimes change or shift unexpectedly. This can result in crews becoming stranded on islands for extended periods of time, or being forced to change course unexpectedly in order to avoid dangerous areas of the New World.

Despite its limitations, the Log Pose is an essential tool for any pirate crew that hopes to find the legendary treasure known as One Piece. The New World is full of mysteries and secrets, and the Log Pose is the only way to navigate through these treacherous waters and discover the secrets that lie hidden on the many islands of the New World.

The Log Pose plays a crucial role in the world of One Piece, both in terms of its practical function as a navigational tool and its symbolic significance as a representation of exploration and discovery. The Log Pose is essential for any pirate crew that hopes to navigate through the dangerous seas of the New World, and it represents the challenge of navigating through the unknown and the rewards that come with the discovery of new islands, new treasures, and new allies.

THE SIGNIFICANCE OF THE PONEGLYPHS AND THEIR TRANSLATION

The Poneglyphs are ancient stone tablets that play a crucial role in the world of One Piece. They are scattered throughout the world, and each one contains information about the history of the world and the ancient kingdom that once ruled it. The Poneglyphs are written in an ancient language that has been lost to time, and they can only be read by a select few individuals who possess the ability to decipher their cryptic messages.

The significance of the Poneglyphs lies in their connection to the ancient kingdom that once ruled the world. The ancient kingdom was a powerful civilization that possessed advanced technology and knowledge far beyond that of any other civilization in the world. The Poneglyphs are the only known records of this ancient kingdom and its history, and they contain information about the true history of the world that has been hidden from the general population for centuries.

The translation of the Poneglyphs is a difficult and dangerous task. The ancient language in which they are written has been lost for centuries, and only a few individuals possess the knowledge and skill required to translate them. Additionally, the World Government has declared the translation of the Poneglyphs to be illegal, and anyone found to be involved in their translation could face severe consequences.

Despite the dangers and challenges involved in their translation, the Poneglyphs are an essential part of the story of One Piece. They are the key to unlocking the secrets of the ancient kingdom and the true history of the world. They also play a significant role in the quest to find the legendary treasure known as One Piece, as it is believed that the location of One Piece is somehow connected to the information contained in the Poneglyphs.

The translation of the Poneglyphs is also closely tied to the concept of freedom and the struggle against tyranny in the world of One Piece. The World Government has declared the translation of the Poneglyphs to be illegal in an attempt to suppress the knowledge contained within them and maintain their hold on power. By translating the Poneglyphs, the characters in One Piece are working to uncover the truth about the world and free it from the grip of the World Government.

The Poneglyphs are a significant and essential part of the world of One Piece. They contain the hidden history of the world and the ancient kingdom that once ruled it, and they play a critical role in the quest to find the legendary treasure known as One Piece. The translation of the Poneglyphs is a dangerous and difficult task, but it is also an important one, as it represents the struggle for freedom and the quest for knowledge and truth in a world dominated by tyranny and secrecy.

THE EVOLUTION OF ONE PIECE'S COMEDY: FROM GAGS TO RUNNING JOKES

One Piece is known for its unique blend of action, adventure, drama, and comedy. Over the years, the series has evolved its approach to humor, moving from simple gags to more elaborate running jokes that have become a trademark of the series. The evolution of One Piece's comedy has been a gradual process, with the series continually experimenting with different types of humor and refining its approach to comedy over time.

In the early years of the series, One Piece relied heavily on physical gags and slapstick humor. Luffy's rubber powers provided ample opportunities for comedic hijinks, and the series frequently used exaggerated reactions and over-the-top physical comedy to elicit laughs from the audience. The humor in these early episodes was often simple and straightforward, designed to provide a quick chuckle or a momentary distraction from the more serious elements of the story.

As the series progressed, the humor in One Piece became more sophisticated and more integrated into the overall narrative. The series began to rely more heavily on running jokes and recurring gags, with certain characters and situations becoming a regular source of humor throughout the series. For example, the character of Usopp became known for his tall tales and his tendency to exaggerate, while Sanji's constant flirtation with women became a recurring theme in the series.

One Piece also began to incorporate more clever wordplay and pop culture references into its humor. Characters would make puns or jokes that played off of common phrases or popular culture, adding an extra layer of humor for those who caught the references. This type of humor added a new dimension to the series, allowing it to appeal to a wider range of viewers and giving the series a more contemporary and relevant feel.

Another significant aspect of One Piece's comedy is the way in which it uses humor to subvert expectations and challenge traditional gender roles and stereotypes. Characters like Nami and Robin are often portrayed as strong and capable women, challenging the traditional portrayal of women in shonen manga as helpless damsels in distress. The series also often pokes fun at traditional gender roles and stereotypes, using humor to highlight the absurdity of these outdated ideas.

Perhaps one of the most significant developments in One Piece's approach to humor is the way in which it uses running jokes and callbacks to previous episodes and story arcs. Characters and situations that were introduced in earlier episodes are often referenced or revisited later in the series, creating a sense of continuity and building a deeper connection between the audience and the characters. This approach to humor allows the series to reward long-time viewers with inside jokes and references, while also making the series more accessible to new viewers by providing context and backstory for the humor.

The evolution of One Piece's comedy has been a gradual and ongoing process, with the series continually experimenting with different types of humor and refining its approach to comedy over time. From simple gags to elaborate running jokes, the series has developed a unique and multifaceted approach to humor that is a key part of its enduring popularity. By incorporating clever wordplay, subverting gender roles, and using running jokes to build a sense of continuity and connection between the audience and the characters, One Piece has created a distinct brand of humor that sets it apart from other shonen manga series.

THE ROLE OF FISHMAN ISLAND AND ITS RELATIONSHIP TO THE SURFACE WORLD

Fishman Island is a significant location in the One Piece universe, both in terms of its cultural significance and its relationship to the surface world. The island is home to a unique society of fishmen and merfolk who have been historically oppressed by humans on the surface world. The island's location at the bottom of the sea makes it a critical gateway to the New World and a vital resource for those seeking to navigate the treacherous waters of the Grand Line.

One of the central themes of Fishman Island is the relationship between fishmen and humans. Throughout the series, fishmen are portrayed as a marginalized and oppressed group, subject to discrimination and violence at the hands of humans. This dynamic is explored in-depth in Fishman Island, with the island serving as a symbol of the struggle for equality and justice for fishmen everywhere.

The island's relationship to the surface world is also a significant aspect of its role in the series. Fishman Island is a critical location for those seeking to navigate the treacherous waters of the Grand Line, as it is home to the only known location of the Sea Forest, a mysterious and dangerous region of the ocean that is essential for navigation in the New World. The island's strategic location also makes it a valuable resource for those seeking to exert control over the seas, with various pirate factions and government forces vying for control of the island and its resources.

One of the key characters in the Fishman Island arc is Fisher Tiger, a legendary pirate who fought for the liberation of fishmen and merfolk. Fisher Tiger's story is emblematic of the struggle for equality and justice that is at the heart of Fishman Island, as he dedicated his life to fighting against the systemic oppression of fishmen and merfolk by humans. His legacy serves as an inspiration to many of the characters in the series, particularly those who have suffered discrimination and marginalization due to their race or species.

The relationship between the fishmen and humans is further explored through the character of Koala, a human who was taken as a slave by the fishmen and subsequently rescued by Fisher Tiger.

Koala's experiences serve as a powerful reminder of the human cost of discrimination and oppression, and her story highlights the importance of empathy and understanding in bridging the divide between different cultures and communities.

Another significant aspect of Fishman Island is its mythology and history. The island is home to ancient ruins and artifacts that hint at a rich and complex history, including the legend of the Sea Kings and the Ancient Weapons. The island's mythology and history are inextricably linked to its relationship with the surface world, as the secrets of the island's past may hold the key to unlocking the mysteries of the New World and cocuring the future of fishmen and merfolk.

Fishman Island plays a significant role in the One Piece universe, both in terms of its cultural significance and its relationship to the surface world. The island serves as a symbol of the struggle for equality and justice for fishmen and merfolk, and its strategic location makes it a critical gateway to the New World. Through its exploration of the relationship between fishmen and humans, the island highlights the importance of empathy and understanding in bridging the divide between different cultures and communities. Its mythology and history also hint at a rich and complex past that is inextricably linked to the island's present and future, making it a fascinating and essential location in the world of One Piece.

THE SIGNIFICANCE OF THE YONKO'S TERRITORIES AND THEIR POWER STRUGGLES

The Yonko, also known as the Four Emperors, are four of the most powerful and notorious pirates in the One Piece world. They are the rulers of the New World and control their own territories. The Yonko include Shanks, Kaido, Big Mom, and Blackbeard. Their territories are home to a variety of other pirate crews and factions that struggle for power and control. The significance of the Yonko's territories and their power struggles cannot be overstated, as they represent some of the biggest threats to the stability of the world of One Piece.

Each Yonko has their own territory, which they have gained through years of piracy and conquest. The territories are vast and diverse, ranging from whole islands to clusters of islands. The territories are heavily fortified, with each Yonko having their own army of loyal followers, making them nearly impenetrable to outsiders. The Yonko rule their territories with an iron fist, using fear and violence to maintain control.

The power struggles between the Yonko are a major source of conflict in the New World. Each Yonko is a formidable opponent in their own right, but when they come into conflict with each other, the results can be catastrophic. These battles can shake the very foundations of the world, and have the potential to drastically alter the balance of power.

For example, when the Yonko Whitebeard died during the Marineford War, it created a power vacuum that led to a scramble for control of his territory. Blackbeard, one of Whitebeard's former crew members, took advantage of this and was able to establish himself as one of the new Yonko. This shift in power had major consequences for the rest of the world, as it led to Blackbeard becoming an even greater threat to stability.

Another example of the power struggles between the Yonko can be seen in the ongoing conflict between Kaido and Big Mom. The two have clashed multiple times, with each trying to gain control over the other's territory. This conflict has the potential to escalate and engulf the entire New World, as other pirate crews and factions are forced to choose sides or risk being caught in the crossfire.

The Yonko's territories and power struggles also have major implications for the world government and the Marines. The government is constantly trying to keep the Yonko in check and prevent them from gaining too much power, while the Marines are tasked with maintaining order and stability in the world. The Yonko represent a major threat to both of these groups, and their territories are considered to be some of the most dangerous places in the world.

The Yonko's territories and power struggles are a crucial element of the One Piece world. They represent a major threat to the stability of the world, and their actions have far-reaching consequences. As the story progresses, it is likely that the Yonko will continue to play a significant role, and their territories will be at the center of some of the biggest conflicts in the series.

THE DIFFERENT TYPES OF CREWS AND THEIR UNIQUE QUALITIES

In the world of One Piece, pirate crews come in many different forms and sizes. Each crew has its own unique qualities that set them apart from other crews, including their goals, methods, and overall personality. Here are some of the different types of crews and their unique qualities:

1. The Straw Hat Pirates: The Straw Hats are the main crew of the One Piece series, and they are known for their close-knit bond and their determination to achieve their goals, no matter what obstacles they face. They are led by Monkey D. Luffy, who has a fierce determination to become the Pirate King, and the rest of the crew is equally passionate about their own personal dreams. They are also known for their diverse range of abilities, which include fighting skills, navigation, and engineering.

2. The Blackbeard Pirates: The Blackbeard Pirates are one of the most notorious crews in the One Piece world. They are led by Marshall D. Teach, also known as Blackbeard, who is known for his ruthless nature and his ambition to become the Pirate King. The crew is made up of some of the most dangerous and unpredictable individuals in the world, and they will stop at nothing to achieve their goals.

3. The Big Mom Pirates: The Big Mom Pirates are led by the powerful and terrifying Big Mom, who rules over her territory with an iron fist. The crew is made up of a wide range of unique individuals, including some of the most powerful devil fruit users in the world. They are known for their love of food, as well as their brutal tactics when it comes to dealing with their enemies.

4. The Whitebeard Pirates: The Whitebeard Pirates were once led by the legendary pirate Whitebeard, who was one of the most powerful individuals in the world. After his death, the crew disbanded, but their legacy lives on. The Whitebeard Pirates were known for their close-knit bond, as well as their sense of loyalty and honor. They were also respected by other crews for their power and their ability to maintain a balance of power in the world.

5. The Heart Pirates: The Heart Pirates are led by Trafalgar Law, who is a skilled surgeon and a powerful devil fruit user. The crew is made up of individuals who have been rescued by Law and are loyal to him because of his compassion and his determination to help those in need. The crew is also known for their strategic thinking and their ability to plan ahead.

6. The Kid Pirates: The Kid Pirates are led by Eustass Kid, who is known for his violent nature and his ambition to become the Pirate King. The crew is made up of some of the most dangerous individuals in the world, and they are not afraid to use violence to achieve their goals. They are also known for their unique and powerful devil fruit abilities.

7. The Red Hair Pirates: The Red Hair Pirates are led by the powerful and respected Shanks, who is one of the few individuals in the world who has the ability to stop a war with just his presence. The crew is known for their loyalty to each other, as well as their sense of honor and respect for other crews. They are also highly respected by the world government and the Marines.

Each crew in the One Piece world has its own unique qualities that make them stand out from other crews. From the Straw Hats' determination to achieve their dreams, to the Blackbeard Pirates' ruthless ambition, each crew has something special that sets them apart. As the series progresses, it will be interesting to see how these different crews interact with each other and how their unique qualities shape the world of One Piece.

THE ROLE OF IMPEL DOWN AND THE WORLD GOVERNMENT'S PRISON SYSTEM

Impel Down is a massive, underwater prison located in the Grand Line, run by the World Government. It is the primary location for holding the most dangerous criminals in the One Piece world, including many infamous pirates and revolutionaries. As the most secure prison in the world, Impel Down plays a significant role in maintaining the balance of power and enforcing the will of the World Government.

Impel Down is divided into several levels, each with its own unique dangers and challenges. The lower levels are the most dangerous, with Level 6 being the most secure and reserved for the most powerful and notorious prisoners. The prisoners are kept in cells and guarded by powerful jailers, making escape nearly impossible. However, there have been a few instances where prisoners have managed to escape, such as the infamous Pirate King, Gol D. Roger, and the former Warlord of the Sea, Crocodile.

The role of Impel Down in the One Piece world is primarily to serve as a deterrent to piracy and to keep dangerous criminals off the streets. The prison system is used to control the most violent and destructive elements in the world, ensuring that the general population is safe from their actions. Additionally, the World Government uses the prison to gather intelligence on criminal organizations and to interrogate prisoners for information.

Impel Down also plays a crucial role in the storyline of One Piece. During the Marineford War, the prison was breached by a group of pirates led by Monkey D. Luffy, who was attempting to rescue his brother, Portgas D. Ace. The prison break was a massive event in the series, as it showed the strength and determination of Luffy and his crew and the lengths they were willing to go to save their loved ones.

The prison system in One Piece is not without its flaws, however. While it is effective in deterring piracy and keeping dangerous criminals off the streets, it also serves as a tool for the World Government to maintain control over the population. Many of the prisoners held in Impel Down are not actually guilty of any crimes but are instead political prisoners who have opposed the World Government in some way. The World Government uses the prison system as a means of silencing dissent and maintaining their grip on power.

Furthermore, the treatment of prisoners in Impel Down is often brutal and inhumane. The jailers are known to use torture to extract information from prisoners, and the conditions in the lower levels of the prison are horrendous. This mistreatment of prisoners is one of the main reasons that the Revolutionary Army opposes the World Government, as they see it as a violation of basic human rights.

The role of Impel Down and the World Government's prison system is to maintain control over the population by deterring piracy, keeping dangerous criminals off the streets, and silencing dissent. While it is effective in achieving these goals, it also has significant flaws, including mistreatment of prisoners and the use of the prison system to silence political opposition.

THE SIGNIFICANCE OF THE TIME-SKIP AND THE STRAW HAT PIRATES' GROWTH

The time-skip in One Piece was a pivotal moment in the series, marking a significant shift in the story and characters. It allowed for a necessary break in the action and introduced a new level of growth and development for the Straw Hat Pirates. In 500 words, we will explore the significance of the time-skip and the growth of the Straw Hat Pirates.

After the events of the Marineford War, the Straw Hat Pirates found themselves in a dire situation. Their captain, Monkey D. Luffy, had suffered a major loss and was unable to protect his crew. They were left with no choice but to separate and train for two years in order to become stronger and reunite. This time-skip allowed for each member to undergo individual growth and development, both physically and mentally.

During the time-skip, each member of the Straw Hat Pirates trained under different mentors to develop their own unique fighting styles and abilities. Luffy trained under Silvers Rayleigh, the former first mate of the Pirate King, to improve his Haki and master Gear Fourth. Zoro trained under Mihawk to hone his swordsmanship and learn to cut through anything. Nami learned how to control the weather and create her own weather systems. Sanji learned to fight with his legs and to use Haki. Chopper learned to control his Monster Point and to use a more advanced form of Rumble Ball. Robin learned how to fight more efficiently and to use her powers in more creative ways. Franky upgraded his cyborg body and weapons. And finally, Brook learned to use ice and to play music that can bring even the dead back to life.

The time-skip also allowed for the Straw Hat Pirates to mentally mature and grow as individuals. They each faced their own personal challenges and overcame them, which resulted in a newfound confidence and sense of purpose. Luffy learned to take on more responsibility as a captain and to strategize before diving into battle. Zoro learned to prioritize the safety of his crew and to not let his own personal ambitions cloud his judgment. Nami learned to trust in her own abilities and to rely on her crew for support. Sanji learned to let go of his anger and to think more rationally.

Chopper learned to stand up for himself and to be more assertive. Robin learned to open up and trust her crewmates. Franky learned to embrace his true identity and to let go of his past. And Brook learned to find joy in life again, even after losing everything he once held dear.

The time-skip also allowed for a shift in the overall tone of One Piece. The series became darker and more mature, with the stakes higher than ever before. The Straw Hat Pirates were no longer just a group of friends going on an adventure; they were a powerful crew with a serious mission. They were now capable of taking on the most dangerous enemies and protecting their loved ones at all costs.

The time-skip was a significant moment in One Piece that allowed for the Straw Hat Pirates to grow and mature in ways that would not have been possible without it. It allowed for each member to develop their own unique abilities and to face personal challenges that resulted in a newfound sense of confidence and purpose. The time-skip also allowed for a shift in the overall tone of the series, setting up higher stakes and a more mature storyline. the time-skip was an essential part of One Piece's evolution and the growth of the Straw Hat Pirates.

ABOUT ETERNIA PUBLISHING

This guide is a result of thorough research from various official sources, including books, courses, biographies, and interviews by renowned experts in the respective fields.

The content is presented in a simplified and practical manner, leaving out redundancies, unnecessary and irrelevant information, and only focusing on the key concepts.

The sources of knowledge are carefully selected and relevant, and the guide aims to provide a broad overview of the reader's topics of interest.

The ultimate goal is to ensure that the text is easily understandable, practical, and pleasant to read.

The reader can acquire a large amount of knowledge from more than one reliable source, making it a useful resource.

The guide is designed to help readers learn and understand specialized information with the greatest effectiveness.

COPYRIGHT

LEGAL DISCLAIMER

This book aims to provide information and entertainment to its readers. The author has used reliable sources for the content, but cannot guarantee its accuracy or validity and is not responsible for any errors or omissions.

The book is not intended to be professional advice and should not replace the guidance of experts. The reader should consult professionals before using any protocols or medical treatments described in the book.

The reader agrees to use the information in the book at their own risk and the author is not liable for any costs, expenses, damages, or professional fees that may arise from using the information in the book. This disclaimer applies to any direct or indirect use of the information, and the author is not liable for any damages, negligence, criminal intent or other causes of action.

REVIEWS

We hope that this book has been helpful in providing a deeper understanding and analysis of the subject.

We appreciate your time in reading and hope that you found the content useful.

If you enjoyed the book, we would be grateful if you could leave a positive review, as this is one of the ways for new authors like us to gain visibility and improve the quality of our writing.

Thank you for your support!

ETERNIA
PUBLISHING